THE BEST OF THE BEST

in Basketball

BY
RACHEL RUTLEDGE

M
THE MILLBROOK PRESS
BROOKFIELD, CONNECTICUT

Produced by
CRONOPIO PUBLISHING
John Sammis, President
and
TEAM STEWART, INC.

Series Design and Electronic Page Makeup by
JAFFE ENTERPRISES
Ron Jaffe

Researched and Edited by
Mark Stewart and Michael Kennedy

All photos courtesy
AP/ Wide World Photos, Inc,
except the following:
Michael Zito/Sports Chrome — Cover

Printed in the United States of America

Published by
The Millbrook Press, Inc.
2 Old New Milford Road
Brookfield, Connecticut   06804

Library of Congress Cataloging-in-Publication Data

Rutledge, Rachel.
  The best of the best in basketball/ by Rachel Rutledge.
  p.   cm.   — (Women of Sports)
  Includes index.
  Summary; Discusses the past and future of women's basketball and presents biographies of
eight of the sport's most famous players: Cynthia Cooper, Teresa Edwards, Lisa Leslie,
Rebecca Lobo, Nikki McCray, Dawn Staley, Kate Starbird, and Sheryl Swoopes.
  ISBN 0-7613-1301-X (lib. bdg.).—ISBN 0-7613-0443-6 (pbk.)
  1. Women basketball players—Biography—Juvenile literature. 2. Basketball for women—
Juvenile literature. [1. Basketball players. 2. Women—Biography. 3. Basketball for women—
History.] I. Title. II. Series: Best of the best in basketball.
GV884.A1R88 1998
796.323'082'0922
[B]—DC21
                                                                                          98-25631
                                                                                          CIP
                                                                                          AC

pbk: 10 9 8 7 6 5 4 3 2 1
lib: 10 9 8 7 6 5 4 3 2 1

CONTENTS

In the Beginning

Grab a few basketball fans on their way out of an ABL, WNBA or NCAA game and ask them to tell you something about the history of women's hoops. You'll get some pretty interesting answers. A lot of folks, for example, believe the college game is just a couple of decades old. Others probably think that women have been playing organized ball only since the 1940s. Imagine their surprise when they learn that women have been playing as long as men: since the early 1890s—before basketball even had a name!

It all started back in the early winter of 1891, when basketball literally sprung from the mind of Dr. James Naismith. He was a physical education instructor at the School for Christian Workers in Springfield, Massachusetts—the "training college" for all YMCA administrative personnel. Like all YMCA workers, Naismith believed that being a "good Christian" meant staying physically fit. In the fall, his students played football, soccer and rugby, and in the spring they ran track and played baseball. But during the winter months, there was little to hold their

Mildred "Babe" Didrikson was the toast of the 1932 Olympics for her track and field exploits. Almost forgotten is that she first made headlines in the 1920s as a schoolgirl basketball star.

interest during the hour they were required to spend in the gymnasium each day. Their choices were limited to calisthenics, tumbling, marching or heaving a medicine ball around—essentially, nothing to stoke their competitive fire.

Naismith's boss, Dr. Luther Gulick, was aware of this problem, and decided that a new indoor sport needed to be invented. After several teachers tried and failed, Gulick assigned this task to Naismith, who was an accomplished multi-sport athlete. The game Naismith devised borrowed from other popular sports of the day, but made the act of scoring safe for indoor play—in other words, there would be no tackling, kicking or overhand throwing. To score a goal in Naismith's game, a player would have to gently lob a soccer ball into a box, which would be nailed to the balcony that encircled the playing floor. A couple of hours before he introduced the new sport to his noon class, he asked the janitor, Pop Stebbins, for a box. The best Pop could do was a round peach basket. Fine, said Naismith, the shape wasn't important.

The good doctor's game was an immediate hit with the students. Soon, almost everyone at the school was playing.

A week or so after the historic first game, word of the new sport (which was as yet unnamed) spread to the nearby Buckingham Grade School. A group of female teachers stopped by the gym on their lunch break and watched from the balcony. They agreed that it would make a fine activity for young ladies, and asked Dr. Naismith if he would teach them how to play. He agreed, and during this tutorial he struck up a relationship with one of the teachers, Maude Sherman. The two ended up getting married.

By 1892, "Basket-Ball" had both a name and a devoted following. It was during this period that two pioneers of the women's game first got involved. Senda Berenson, the physical education director at Smith College, believed that basketball was an ideal sport for young women. Berenson was something of a radical. At a time when almost everyone believed that physical exertion was bad for women, she believed that it was what they most needed. She was, however, concerned that basketball might be too rough for her students. Berenson did not want them smashing into one another, as the men often did, nor did she like the idea that a defensive player could snatch the ball away from an opponent. It just wasn't "ladylike." In fact, when she authored the official women's basketball rules for Spalding in 1899, stealing was *outlawed*. Also, to limit the area players had to cover, Berenson divided the court into three sections, and no player was allowed to leave her area.

The first female professional team began play in 1915, and they called themselves the Edmonton Commercial Grads. As the name implied, they were graduates of a commercial high school in the Canadian province of Alberta. They played in Canada, the United States and Europe, and once won 147 games in a row.

In the United States, the driving force behind women's basketball was the Amateur Athletic Union, which began holding tournaments and selecting All-America teams in the mid-1920s. The best AAU clubs were those sponsored by organizations that encouraged their female employees

Carol Blazejowski (#8) put women's college basketball on the map in the 1970s. She scored a record 3,199 points for Montclair State, and later starred for the New Jersey Gems in the first women's pro league.

to form company teams. These teams competed against one another on a regional basis, boosting worker morale and giving the companies with the best squads tremendous publicity. Sometimes a company would go out of its way to hire a woman it knew was an accomplished ball player, even if a legitimate job did not exist.

This was how a wiry 13-year-old girl from Beaumont, Texas, came to work as a typist for the Employers Casualty Company in 1928. Mildred Didrikson was already well known in Texas as the finest schoolgirl player anyone had ever seen. With a dream of becoming the greatest athlete in history—and no real competition in high school—she eagerly joined Employers Casualty, which sponsored women's teams in several sports. While with the company, Didrikson did a little typing and a lot of winning, taking titles in track, swimming, and ice skating, and setting a world record in the javelin throw. She also led the Golden Cyclones to the AAU basketball championship in 1931. "Babe," as everyone called her, went on to make headlines in the 1932 Olympics, winning medals in every event she entered.

In the years just prior to World War II, Alline Banks Sprouse emerged as the best player in the country. A 5-10 forward with a great shooting touch, she played for several company teams in the south during the 1930s and 1940s, and was voted the AAU's top player nine times. The better her opponents, the better Sprouse played. In an All-Star game held in New York's Madison Square Garden, she scored an unheard-of 56 points.

During the 1950s and 60s, the "queen of the courts" was Nera White, who earned All-America honors 15 times. Playing for the Nashville Business College, she led the team to 10 AAU titles, and was named the tournament MVP 10 times. More important than her countless trophies was that White narrowed the gap between men and women. She could do all of the things that female players were not supposed to be able to do, such as dribbling around opponents, powering her way to the basket, or pulling up and popping a classic jumper.

White's eye-opening skills began to open some minds, too. When she began, the women's game was still incredibly restrictive. From 1949 to 1961, for instance, the rules allowed only two dribbles before a player had to pass or shoot, and from 1961 to 1966 a payer could only bounce the ball three times. Not until the 1966-67 season did unrestricted dribbling come to women's basketball. That same year, all players were allowed to leave their "zones" and go the length of the floor for the first time.

Finally, in the 1971-72 season, women's basketball assumed its present form, with five-on-five full-court action. Something the women's game had at the time that the men's game did *not* was a 30-second shot clock. First introduced in 1969 on an experimental basis, it sped up the action and gave a huge advantage to women who could create shots for themselves.

The first college player to command national attention was Carol

Ann Meyers was the first female athlete to earn a full scholarship to UCLA. She grew up playing ball with her brother, Dave, who was a top player for the UCLA men's team and later an All-Star in the NBA.

Blazejowski of Montclair State College, in New Jersey. She learned basketball playing in pickup games near her home in Cranford, and did not

actually join her high school varsity until she was a senior. By then, she had a fully developed set of skills that completely transcended the still-developing girls' game. "Blaze" was unstoppable in college, regularly pouring in 30 to 40 points a night. In 1977, she gave the sport a glimpse of its future when she drew 12,000-plus fans to Madison Square Garden for a game against Queens College, then treated them to an electrifying 52-point performance.

Others who laid the foundation for the current college game included Ann Meyers (UCLA), Nancy Lieberman, Ann Donovan (Old Dominion) and Lynette Woodard (Kansas).

Any of these stars could have held her own against the best collegians of the 1990s, but the woman who ultimately cast the die for the modern player was Cheryl Miller. At 6' 3" she had the size and the post-up game to dominate in the paint. But she was also a silky smooth ballhandler and a deadly shooter. Indeed, during four All-American seasons at the University of Southern California, Miller was practically unguardable. She had a basketball-playing brother against whom she could hone her skills (NBA star Reggie Miller), and combined size with her speed and all-around skills. Plus, she brought an aggressive attitude to the court. She "walked the walk and talked the talk"—and was even known to throw one down every once in a while!

The stars of the 1970s and early 80s boosted the popularity of women's basketball to new heights. But they were part of an even bigger picture. During this time, the demographics of America shifted dramatically. Women were entering the workplace in unprecedented numbers, and had more spendable income, more decision-making power and more leisure time than ever before. What entrepreneurs and sports marketing experts saw in these emerging trends was a real possibility for women's professional basketball. In 1978, the first such attempt was made, with the formation of the Women's Professional Basketball League. The WPBL

Nancy Lieberman (right), who learned to play basketball on the outdoor courts of New York City, was a college star at Old Dominion. She led the Lady Monarchs to two national championships.

limped along for a few years, and made occasional headlines by offering huge salaries to the likes of Meyers and Blazejowski, but it folded when attendance bottomed out.

Thus for more than a decade, the best college players had to make an uncomfortable choice after graduation. They could continue playing top-level basketball—if they were willing to live and work in a European country—or they could stay at home and compete (with little or no compensation) for the national team in the Pan Am Games, Goodwill Games, World Championships of Basketball, and the Olympics. Choosing the latter meant having to earn a living as a coach or in some other job. Players used to competing in 30 to 50 games a year generally found the inactivity unbearable, and went overseas to play pro ball.

Fortunately, the news was not all bad for American women. After years of watching the Soviets walk away with top international honors, the U.S. team began striking back. America won Olympic gold in 1984, and again in '88, to assert its dominance on the world scene. Meanwhile, the NCAA was working tirelessly to promote its top stars and teams. In 1993, the Women's Final Four was a sellout for the first time, and in 1994 the national championship was decided on a long-range buzzer-beater by North Carolina's Charlotte Smith. Television ratings and attendance soared during the 1990s, proving that money could be made if women's ball was marketed correctly. Slowly but surely, plans were laid to form a professional league.

The target year was 1996. With the Olympics being held in Atlanta and the men's national team a virtual lock to win a gold medal, the eyes of America's basketball fans would be on the women. If they won the gold, there would be enough interest and plenty of money to sponsor a pro circuit. If they lost, however, pro basketball might not get off the ground. In preparation for Atlanta, USA Basketball began assembling and training the Olympic team in 1995. Many top players turned down six-figure salaries from foreign teams to "invest" a year of their lives in this cause.

By the time the Olympics rolled around, Team USA was functioning like a well-oiled machine, and the individual players were familiar to millions of fans. They won the gold in convincing fashion.

The national team's easy triumph in Atlanta generated such enthusiasm that *two* pro leagues were formed: the American Basketball League and the Women's National Basketball Association. At first, critics claimed that two organizations would drive up salaries, divide interest and cause the downfall of both leagues. But after two seasons, the ABL and WNBA were in far better shape than anyone could have imagined. The following chapters focus on key players in both leagues. Some are part of the "old guard" of women's basketball, while others represent the future of the sport. Together they will define where it goes and how it gets there.

Cheryl Miller, a four-time All-American at USC in the 1980s, set the standard for today's top players. She combined quickness, size, power, and agility. And like her brother, Reggie, she loved to make the big shot in the big game.

"The dumbest question is the question you don't ask. If you don't understand something really try to communicate."

Cynthia Cooper

As a rule, great basketball players are born, not made. The talent is there, waiting to be coaxed out of them at an early age. Then it is honed to a fine edge through years of coaching and practice. Cynthia Cooper had this greatness within her, yet no one—including Cynthia herself—had a clue it was there.

Indeed, her path to stardom was anything but direct. Born in Chicago and raised in the Watts section of Los Angeles, Cynthia was the youngest of eight children being raised by Mary Cobbs, a single mother. There was rarely the time or the opportunity for basketball when she was little—the schoolyards of Watts are no place for a young girl. Looking back on her childhood, though, Cynthia realizes the lessons she learned before she ever set foot on a court served her well once she started playing ball in ninth grade.

"You have to grow up fast in that kind of environment," she says. "If you don't, it could be detrimental to your health! I think my experiences helped me to be mentally as well as physically tough, and able to meet some major challenges and demands I have been faced with."

Cynthia first came to basketball as an escape. "I wanted to get into some kind of physical activity that would interest me and keep me off the streets," Cynthia recalls. Why basketball? "I started because I saw a young lady put the ball behind her back and then make a layup. I thought I'd like to learn how to do that."

When Cynthia Cooper arrived in Houston, she was expected to be a role player. She ended up leading the Comets to the WNBA title.

Cynthia Cooper and guard Tammi Reiss of the Utah Starzz enjoy a job well done during the WNBA's All-Star 2-ball competition at New York's Madison Square Garden.

Needless to say, Cynthia had a lot of catching up to do. She went out for the Locke High School team, competing against girls who had been playing organized ball for years. Luckily, Cynthia's natural ability and eagerness to learn caught the eye of coach Art Webb, a legendary teacher and motivator, who knew a diamond in the rough when he saw one. Cynthia exceeded even her coach's lofty expectations, however, when she became Los Angeles's Player of the Year during her senior season. Behind her 31 points per game, Locke won the California state championship. From there, she accepted a scholarship to the University of Southern California.

Like most student-athletes, Cynthia had a difficult time adjusting to college life her freshman year. "When I started at USC I don't think I was quite ready to juggle schoolwork, practice, games and time for myself," she recalls. "It wasn't easy learning to put all the pieces of the puzzle together." As always, her solution to the problem was simply to work harder. And if she did not understand something in class, or had a hard time with a concept on the basketball court, she did the smart thing: she raised her hand and asked. Cynthia finished the 1981-82 campaign with a 14.6 scoring average, and was named a Freshman All-American. Her next two seasons were even more rewarding, as she teamed with Cheryl

Miller to guide USC to back-to-back national championships. Miller may have been the marquee superstar for the Women of Troy, but it was Cynthia who kept the team loose and provided a special kind of leadership. When asked about Cynthia, her coach at USC, Linda Sharp, liked to say that her upbeat attitude and tireless work ethic added a unique dimension to the team. It kept the USC players cohesive when the pressures of playing for a championship could have torn the team apart.

In the days before women's professional basketball took hold in the United States, the top college players actually had to leave the country in order to advance to the next level and earn a living in the game. When Cynthia graduated from USC in 1986, she decided to continue her career in Spain. The thought of leaving her mother troubled her, but she just could not pass up the opportunity to play professionally. Thus began an 11-year odyssey, during which Cynthia established herself as one of the finest players in the world. Nine times during that period she led her team in scoring, and in 1987 she was named Most Valuable Player of the European All-Star Game. In 1996, her last season away from the U.S., Cynthia shot out the lights at the prestigious European Cup tournament, averaging more than 37 points per game.

At the 1988 Olympics, Cynthia helped the Americans win by playing solid defense and contributing 14 points a game. Cynthia stood beside her teammates as they waited to accept their gold medals, and began thinking about how far she had come since her days in Watts. She

Getting Personal

Cynthia was born in Chicago, Illinois on April 14, 1963...She was the youngest of eight kids...Between seasons in high school, Cynthia developed her game by playing against boys...Cynthia used her speed and jumping ability to star for the Locke High School track team. She held the national high school record for the fastest time in the 330-meter hurdles...Cynthia majored in Physical Education at USC...She says she treats people the way she would like to be treated, except on the court—"but that's basketball," she smiles.

17

Career *Highlights*

Year	Team	Honor
1981	Locke High School	L.A. High School Player of the Year
1981	Locke High School	California State Champion
1982	USC	Freshman All-American
1983	USC	National Champion
1984	USC	National Champion
1986	USC	NCAA All-Tournament
1988	Parma (Italy)	Three-Point Shooting Champion
1988	Team USA	Olympic Gold Medalist
1992	Parma (Italy)	Three-Point Shooting Champion
1992	Team USA	Olympic Bronze Medalist
1997	Comets	WNBA Scoring Champion & MVP
1997	Comets	WNBA Champion and Playoff MVP

thought about her brother, Everett, who had died three years earlier, consumed by the same streets from which she had managed to escape. Then Cynthia spotted her mother, sitting in the stands, as proud as can be. "That was one of the greatest and saddest moments of my career," she recalls. "Three years after Everett was buried, I won my first Olympic gold medal and he wasn't there to share it with me. But it was the 29th of September, my mother's birthday. She was there, and I got to present her with the gold medal."

Today, Cynthia is a star in the WNBA. She had a great first year, winning the MVP and leading the Houston Comets to the league title. When she hangs up her sneakers, she wants to coach. She will bring to her young players a keen understanding of basketball, and a success story that ranks among the most inspiring in all of sports. And she will also serve as an example of just how much a talented player can accomplish if she is willing to work hard and never lose faith in her own abilities. As Cynthia likes to say, "It's been a struggle to get to where I am today, and I don't take anything for granted. I never doubted myself. I've always had confidence in my game."

Though in her mid-30s, Cynthia has lost none of her speed or desire.

On Her Mind

"I haven't allowed myself to look back yet, because there is so much more I want to accomplish."

Teresa Edwards

I f you're not going to do it right—and do it hard—don't do it at all." As a young girl, Teresa Edwards heard those words from her mother, Mildred. Teresa kept them close to her heart through all her years as a basketball gypsy, and they served her well. No one in the sport has traveled a tougher road—or accomplished more—than she has.

Teresa began her hoops career in Cairo, Georgia. She spent countless hours playing with her four sports-crazy brothers, shooting at an old bicycle rim nailed to a pine tree in their front yard. Her first opportunity to play with other girls came in the seventh grade. She wanted to try out for the Washington Middle School team, but her mother said no. Mildred, a single mother who worked multiple jobs to support her kids, did not want her baby girl to waste her education playing a game.

Teresa defied her mother and went out for the team without telling her. Mildred finally caught on a few weeks later when she began lobbying for a pair of new sneakers. Furious at first, Mildred changed her mind once she saw Teresa in action. Teresa was a glorious player, and that made her proud. Besides, she thought, basketball might open doors to other things. Mildred never missed a game after that.

In 1997, Teresa became the first player-coach in pro basketball in more than 20 years.

Teresa understands the importance of connecting with her fans.

Teresa's play continued to improve as she joined the Cairo High School varsity, and she earned All-America recognition as a senior. She had quick hands, an explosive first step, tremendous court vision, and an understanding of the game that a lot of college stars did not possess. Among the many recruiters Teresa impressed was Andy Landers, who coached the women's basketball team for the University of Georgia. He offered her a full scholarship and she accepted.

In four years, Teresa led the University of Georgia to three Southeastern Conference championships, and was a First-Team All-American in her junior and senior years. As a sophomore she made the U.S. Olympic squad, and played a supporting role in Team USA's 1984 gold medal victory. Needless to say, after graduation Teresa wanted to continue playing basketball.

Getting Personal

Teresa was born on July 19, 1964 in Cairo, Georgia—the birthplace of baseball star Jackie Robinson...Teresa's four brothers shared one bedroom in their small house, while she and her mom shared another..."There's no mom like my mom," she boasts. "They don't make them like that anymore."...Teresa was the youngest member of the 1984 U.S. Olympic team, and the oldest member of the 1996 squad...What's the next step for women's pro ball? According to Teresa, players must learn how to entertain. "Women are still playing basic basketball," she says. "The next level for us is to play more creative basketball, and that is where we have to learn from men."

The year was 1986, and the only place to make a decent living in women's ball was in Europe. Teresa did not like the idea of leaving the country. "I'm an American girl," she says. "I like hot dogs and fast food." When she thought about her mother's words, however, she knew she had to go. She signed with a team in the Italian League and said *arriva derci* to her friends and family.

Teresa became a star in Europe, but she was all but forgotten in the United States. That changed in 1988, when she made headlines at the Olympics in Seoul, South Korea. Teresa led the women's team to the gold medal, averaging 16 points a game and leading everyone in steals and assists.

In 1989 a team from Japan offered her a large contract to play basketball. The money was significantly better than she could have made at a job in the U.S., and a lot more than she had made as a pro in Italy. Teresa knew it could help her family, and she decided to go. "What are you living for," she asks, "if you can't provide somebody with a better way of life?"

Teresa performed brilliantly over the next seven years, both in Japan and in Europe, regularly scoring between 30 and 40 points a game. She became widely recognized by the international basketball community as the top player in the world. In 1995 Teresa returned to the United States to join Team USA, which had scheduled a 52-game international tour in preparation for the 1996 Olympics in Atlanta. She was appointed team co-captain, and often functioned as an on-the-floor coach. Team USA

Career HIGHLIGHTS

Year	Team	Achievement
1982	Cairo H.S.	High School All-American
1984	Georgia	First-Team All-SEC
1984	Team USA	Olympic Gold Medalist
1985	Georgia	First-Team All-SEC
1985	Georgia	First-Team All-American
1986	Georgia	First-Team All-SEC
1986	Georgia	First-Team All-American
1988	Team USA	Olympic Gold Medalist
1992	Team USA	Olympic Bronze Medalist
1996	Team USA	Olympic Gold Medalist
1997	Atlanta Glory	ABL All-Star
1998	Atlanta Glory	ABL All-Star

came together on the tour—going undefeated—and rolled into Atlanta for the '96 games as a huge favorite. But prior to the opening game, point guard Dawn Staley went down with an injury. The responsibility for running the offense suddenly fell to Teresa, who had been the team's shooting guard. Summoning all she had learned since first playing the point at Georgia, Teresa guided Team USA flawlessly. She controlled the tempo of every game, and averaged eight assists per contest. After defeating Brazil in the final, Teresa collected her third Olympic gold medal.

In the fall of 1996, Teresa was very much in demand. Two new leagues were forming and both wanted her badly. She signed with the American Basketball League's Atlanta Glory. Finally, after all these years, Teresa could do her thing at home!

As Teresa moves into the final years of her career, she may become an even more valuable asset to women's basketball. The thing a new league needs most is respected, experienced people who have both solid ties with the past and an understanding of what lies ahead in the future. Teresa provides that and more. And she also has some sage advice to pass along to those who would challenge her records: "If you're not going to do it right—and do it hard—don't do it at all."

Kansas guard Tamecka Dixon, left, tries to steal the ball from Teresa during the U.S. National Team competition in 1995.

ON HER MIND
"It pushes me to do bigger and better things when I think about how kids look up to me and my achievements."

Lisa Leslie

When you are six feet tall in the seventh grade, you get kind of tired of everyone asking if you play basketball. Lisa Leslie certainly did. Basketball had always been just another game to her, but because of the annoying questions she was beginning to hate it. Lisa, in fact, was about to quit altogether. But then a friend talked her into trying out for the junior high team, and that changed everything. Lisa played center for the first time, and she really enjoyed being in the middle of the action. The team went 7-0 and she was hooked. Lisa loved being part of a team, she liked the closeness and she discovered she had a real competitive fire. "I guess it was my destiny," she smiles.

Closeness and teamwork were nothing new to Lisa. When she was four years old her father left home, and that meant she, her mom and two sisters had to function as a team. Rather than working several low-paying jobs, or going on welfare, Christine Leslie decided to go into business for herself. She scraped up enough money for a down payment on an 18-wheeler and became a trucker. During the school year, Lisa's mom was often away for weeks at a time, and she missed her terribly. Christine hired a live-in housekeeper, but each girl had specific chores to do, and it took a lot of cooperation to keep the house running smoothly. "It made me mature really fast," Lisa says. "I had so much to do."

Lisa is one of the WNBA's most recognizable players.

Lisa has the city of Los Angeles psyched to watch women's basketball. Her presence in the middle for the Sparks makes her—both literally and figuratively—the team's center of attention.

During the summers, Lisa and her sister Tiffany would accompany Christine on her long hauls. They slept side-by-side in the cramped little cab behind the driver's compartment, and ate at truck stops all over the country. In other words, they had a blast! Each summer, however, the sleeping arrangements got a little tighter, as Lisa kept growing and growing.

By the time she entered Morningside High School in Los Angeles, she was well over six feet tall. Lisa began to sense that her future was in basketball, and worked hard to improve her game. She learned to use her size against smaller opponents, but realized that as she advanced to each level she would have to do more than just be tall. Lisa worked with her cousin, Craig, to develop her footwork and shooting, and practiced her open-court moves at the local playground. To improve her stamina she did sit-ups and push-ups, and also played pick-up games for hours on end.

Lisa made the Morningside varsity as a freshman and started every game. By her junior season she stood 6' 5" and was the top schoolgirl ballplayer in L.A. Off the court, she starred in volleyball and track. And all through high school she maintained excellent grades. Lisa knew that sports would lead to a college scholarship, but she also understood that she had to "learn how to learn" in order to take advantage of a university education.

Lisa's senior season was one for the books. No one could stop her, as she averaged more than 27 points and 15 rebounds a game. In one game, Lisa scored 101 points in one half, and the other team refused to come out and finish the game!

Getting Personal

Lisa was born to Christine Leslie on July 7, 1972, in Los Angeles, California....Her mom is 6-3...Lisa patterned her game after James Worthy of the L.A. Lakers. "Whenever the Lakers needed a basket, they would give it to 'Big Game James.' When I'd watch him, I'd say, 'One day I want to be that kind of player.'"...She was honored as the USA Basketball Female Athlete of the Year in 1993...What is Lisa's take on dunking? "Dunking is something guys care more about than girls," she maintains. "There's something about jumping that seems to fascinate guys. Girls are more, like, 'As long as the ball goes in, who cares how you got it there?'"

When the college scholarship offers came pouring in, Lisa decided to stay close to home. She opted for the University of Southern California, an excellent school with one of the top hoops programs in the country. In her first game for the Women of Troy, Lisa scored 30 points and grabbed 20 rebounds. She also stunned crowds during warmups by dunking the basketball. "I've been able to dunk since I was in the ninth grade because of a technique I learned doing the high jump in track," Lisa says, adding that she never did it during games. "It's more dangerous for women because other women aren't used to being dunked on, so sometimes they

Career Highlights

Year	Team	Achievement
1990	Morningside H.S.	USA Today Player of the Year
1991	USC	NCAA Freshman of the Year
1991	USC	First-Team All-PAC 10
1992	USC	Second-Team All-American
1992	USC	First-Team All-PAC 10
1993	USC	First-Team All-American
1993	USC	First-Team All-PAC 10
1994	USC	First-Team All-American
1994	USC	First-Team All-PAC 10
1994	USC	College Player of the Year
1996	Team USA	Olympic Gold Medalist
1997	Sparks	First-Team All-WNBA
1997	Sparks	WNBA Rebounding Champion
1998	Team USA	Gold Medalist, World Championships

accidentally undercut you." Lisa had superb sophomore and junior seasons at USC, and greatly improved her defense. In her senior year, she blossomed into the nation's best player.

In 1995, Lisa joined Team USA and began to prepare for the '96 Olympics. Team USA's guards and forwards had no rivals on the international scene, but the center position was a different story. There were a lot of big, tough women who knew how to clog the middle and dominate on the boards. Lisa was the team's only "true" center, so it was imperative that she learn how best to use her skills to nullify her bulkier and more experienced opponents. If she failed, the consequences could have been disastrous.

By the time the team reached Atlanta, Lisa was ready. She played wonderfully, and so did her teammates, as Team USA won their first five games against Cuba, Ukraine, Zaire, Australia, and South Korea. In the semifinals, Lisa shot out the lights, scoring 35 points against Japan. During the gold medal game, Lisa allowed Brazil's center to establish inside position too easily. Coach Tara VanDerveer decided it was time for a wake-up call. She pulled Lisa out of the game.

Lisa got the message: play defense or someone else will. When she re-entered the game, she dominated at both ends of the court, enabling Team USA to pull away in the second half for a 111-87 victory. Lisa ended up as high scorer, with 29 points on remarkable 12-for-14 shooting. When it came right down to it, she had played her best in the biggest game of her life.

In 1997, Lisa established herself as the WNBA's top center, and was honored as a First-Team All-Star. She also led the league in rebounding, with 9.5 per game. "The WNBA is a dream come true," says Lisa. "I always wanted to play pro basketball—not in Europe, not in Japan—but pro basketball in the USA. I think with the Olympics and the WNBA, maybe my success has surpassed my childhood dreams."

Lisa skies against North Carolina State University during Team USA's 52-game international tour.

ON HER MIND

"My life is not completely normal, but I make sure I find the time for my family and friends and always make sure I have time for myself."

Rebecca Lobo

Get meaner. *Take control.* When a coach growls these commands at a star player, the player is supposed to respond with flying elbows and an in-your-face attitude. But what if it goes against everything that the player has ever believed in? What if it goes against everything that has worked for her in the past? This was the dilemma Rebecca Lobo faced during her senior year at the University of Connecticut. She was the nation's most celebrated college player, on the country's most dominant team. All that eluded the Huskies was a national championship, and coach Geno Auriemma was looking for Rebecca to get tough and take the team all the way. "But that's not my nature," she smiles.

Indeed, ever since Rebecca first picked up a basketball, she has been a real "Mrs. Nice Guy." That has a lot to do with how Dennis and RuthAnn Lobo raised her. Rebecca was encouraged to love, support and depend on her siblings, Rachel and Jason. Among the many things they shared was an intense love of sports. RuthAnn, who had been a good high school basketball player, encouraged them to excel in athletics. They played stickball, wiffleball, volleyball, soccer and even boxed together. Rebecca remembers squatting behind home plate—in catcher's equipment made out of newspaper and a football helmet—when Jason threw batting practice to Rachel.

During Rebecca's senior year at Southwick-Tolland Regional High School, she became one of the most celebrated and recognizable athletes in Massachusetts. She had grown to 6' 4", a size that enabled her to dominate games at both ends of the court. Most players dream about scoring

Rebecca led the New York Liberty to the 1997 WNBA finals in her first pro season.

33

30 points and grabbing 20 rebounds in a game. Rebecca actually averaged better than that over the course of the 1990-91 season. She finished her high school career with 2,596 points to establish a new state record.

When it came time to choose a college, she had her pick of over 100. Rebecca chose the University of Connecticut, which was about an hour south of her home. She had always counted on the support of her family, and with the campus so close she knew her parents would be able to attend all of her home games.

The Rebecca Lobo Era of UConn basketball started with much fanfare, but little in the way of results. In her first college game she looked confused and overmatched, and managed just 10 points before fouling out. "I didn't have a clue what college basketball was about," she admits. But as always, she found the silver lining in the dark cloud. "I knew it couldn't get any worse."

She was right. Rebecca rebounded from her inauspicious debut to earn Rookie of the Year honors in the Big East Conference. The following season she was selected first-team All-Big East—an honor she would earn a total of three times. After her junior year, in 1994, she garnered two new awards. First she was chosen the Big East Women's Basketball Scholar Athlete of the Year, and was also named a first-team All-American.

The trophies and plaques were nice, but Rebecca knew her college career would not be complete without an NCAA championship. History is littered with great players who failed to win. Some simply

Rebecca transformed UConn into a national powerhouse.

came along at the wrong time, while others never had the right supporting cast. But the mark of a great player is the ability to make those around you better, and Rebecca definitely saw herself as someone who could be that kind of star. The only problem was that Coach Auriemma expected her to do it one way, while she had something very different in mind.

Eventually, Rebecca found a happy medium. She did not "demand the ball" every trip down the floor, as Auriemma wanted, but she did work hard to establish good position whenever the Huskies had possession. The mere threat of Rebecca getting a pass near the basket was enough to send opponents into a state of confusion, and this gave her teammates the openings they needed. The guards could penetrate, the forwards could slash to the basket, and someone was bound to be open.

Getting Personal

Rebecca was born to RuthAnn and Dennis Lobo in Southwick, Massachusetts on October 6, 1973...Her brother's name is Jason and her sister's name is Rachel...Growing up, Rebecca rooted for the Boston Celtics and loved watching the duels between Julius Erving and Larry Bird...Her favorite baseball player was Carlton Fisk...When she was 10, she wrote a letter to Boston Celtics General Manager Red Auerbach, predicting she would be the first woman to play for the team...Rebecca's extra-curricular activities in high school included a stint in the school band.

Sometimes that person was Rebecca, who was immediately double- and triple-teamed. She would wait patiently until she saw an open teammate, and then whip the ball to them for an uncontested shot. Rebecca's scoring suffered, but her assists soared. More important, UConn was winning everything in sight. Game after game, opposing coaches would tell reporters, "Well, at least we didn't let Lobo beat us." Rebecca knew better. She was *murdering* them. And best of all, she had found a happy medium between what Coach Auriemma wanted and what she believed was best for her. The Huskies went undefeated that season, and swept through the NCAA Tournament to claim the 1995 national championship.

Career HIGHLIGHTS

Year	Team	Achievement
1991	Southwick-Tolland	Parade H.S. All-American
1991	Southwick-Tolland	Mass. Player of the Year
1992	UConn	Big East Rookie of the Year
1994	UConn	Big East Player of the Year
1995	UConn	First-Team All-American
1995	UConn	Final Four MVP
1995	UConn	NCAA National Champion
1995	UConn	National Player of the Year
1996	Team USA	Olympic Gold Medalist
1997	New York Liberty	Second-Team All-WNBA

In the spring of 1995, with her diploma in hand, Rebecca faced the same decision every college basketball star had for nearly two decades: play for money in Europe, or turn the page on basketball and get on with your life. Luckily for Rebecca, she had a third option. When she received an invitation to try out for Team USA and play in the 1996 Summer Olympics, she jumped at the opportunity.

Rebecca made the team, but was hardly its star. True, she was the most famous player in America. But she had a long way to go before she could hold her own against savvy international veterans like Cynthia Cooper and Teresa Edwards. As Rebecca saw it, this was *still* a dream come true. She knew that if a starter was injured or got into foul trouble, she would be thrust into the spotlight and expected to shine. The team did better than anyone could have imagined on its pre-olympic tour, going 52-0. That meant Rebecca had gone nearly two years without experiencing a defeat!

That streak was kept alive during the Olympics, as Team USA rolled over its opponents and captured the gold medal. The women's game had taken a huge step in terms of quality and competitiveness, and millions of Americans witnessed this magic moment on television.

After the Games, it was announced that two new professional leagues would be formed: the American Basketball League and the Women's National Basketball Association. The WNBA wanted a strong team in

A veteran of top-level NCAA and Olympic competition, Rebecca oozes confidence.

New York, and a well-known player to anchor that franchise. The Liberty signed Rebecca to a generous contract, and surrounded her with a group of quality players, including forwards Vickie Johnson and Kym Hampton, and guard Teresa Weatherspoon. As an NCAA champion and gold medalist, Rebecca also served as a spokesperson for the WNBA, and be the initial focal point for fans and the press in the New York area. The Liberty came together beautifully and made it all the way to the WNBA finals, with everyone contributing.

Of her amazing unbeaten run, her great 1997 season, and her position at the forefront of women's basketball, Rebecca says that the important thing is not how it benefits her, but hopefully how it affects others. "It's good that girls can see a woman playing," Rebecca says, "and look to her as a role model."

ON HER MIND

"My bread and butter is being able to create and shoot off the dribble."

Nikki McCray

In the 1960s, Rick Barry said "nuts" to the NBA to play in the American Basketball Association. In the 1970s, Bobby Hull blew off the NHL to star in the World Hockey Association. And in the 1980s, Heisman Trophy winners Herschel Walker, Doug Flutie and Mike Rozier sidestepped the NFL for a shot at big bucks in the United States Football League. Perhaps it is a sign of the times that, in the 1990s, the athlete most associated with league-jumping is probably Nikki McCray, the quicksilver guard who followed her MVP season in the American Basketball League by signing with the WNBA. It was not so long ago that no one would have even cared. But thanks to players like Nikki, women's basketball is now a big-time pro sport.

A few years back, Nikki was a sensation for the University of Tennessee. As the cornerstone of coach Pat Summitt's great teams of the mid-1990s, McCray was the college game's most compelling two-way player. On defense, she was given the job of locking up and shutting down an opponent's best scorer. On offense, she was the nation's top penetrator. And in transition, she was absolutely unstoppable. As good as Nikki was, however, she ached to improve. Little did she know how much or how fast she would accomplish these goals.

Nikki was born and raised in Colliersville, Tennessee. The oldest of four kids, she was known less for her basketball skills than her beautiful singing voice. She came to basketball in the ninth grade. Taller than most

WNBA President Val Ackerman welcomes Nikki to the league.

Nikki poses in front of Italy's picturesque Lake Como during a tour of Europe.

girls and gifted with tremendous speed and anticipation, she says the sport seemed totally natural to her from the first time she participated in an organized game.

As a member of the varsity, Nikki began to develop her trademark move. Starting at the perimeter, she would throw a fake at a defender to get her off-balance, then explode in the other direction. If there was no one in the middle she continued right to the basket, where she either attempted a layup or laid the ball off to an open teammate. If her path was blocked, however, she would head for the right baseline. From there, Nikki was absolutely deadly. She spent hours practicing her baseline jumper knowing that most defenders would try to force her to that spot. Normally a low-percentage shot, Nikki actually made that play her specialty. By her senior season, Nikki was the most well-known player in the state. She earned high school All-America honors from *Parade Magazine* and *USA Today*, and was offered what every schoolgirl basketball star in Tennessee dreams of: a scholarship to UT.

At Tennessee, Nikki was counted upon to be the team's sparkplug. But a devastating knee injury almost ended her college career before it even started. She tore her anterior cruciate ligament in 1990 and had to sit

out the entire 1990-91 season. Nikki
worked hard to rebuild her knee, and
by the 1992-93 campaign it was as
good as new. Meanwhile, all of the
rehabbing had made her bigger,
stronger, and faster. In her four seasons
with the Lady Vols, Nikki improved
each year, and each year the team
advanced to the NCAA Tournament.
In all, Tennessee won 122 of 133
games with Nikki on the floor.

After graduating in 1995, Nikki
looked forward to the next challenge:
making the Olympic team.

That dream nearly turned into a
nightmare for Nikki. The combination
of playing, traveling and surviving

Getting Personal

Nikki was born in Colliersville, Tennessee on
December 17, 1971...Her first sports idols
were the Dallas Cowboys Cheerleaders, but
after watching Florence Griffith Joyner's
gold-medal performance at the 1988
Olympics, Nikki had a new favorite...She
thinks her game most closely resembles that
of multitalented NBA star Scottie
Pippen...What makes Nikki an MVP-caliber
performer? "I take a lot of pride in my
defense," she says. "That's always going to
be there because it's natural. But I think I've
improved a lot in my three-point
shooting."...Nikki's newest hobby is jet-
skiing...Nikki has a very precise pre-game
ritual. She eats pasta with meat sauce, takes
a short nap, then jumps in the shower
before heading over to the arena.

Coach Tara VanDerveer's super-tough practices began to reveal the limi-
tations in Nikki's game. She never had much use for an outside shot in
college, thanks to her amazing driving ability. But against more experienced opponents—who did not always nibble at her fakes, and knew how
to play solid team defense—her effectiveness was greatly limited.
Frustrated, she tried to do too much when she was handling the ball, and
started committing turnovers.

Then it happened. During a game in which Nikki had lost the ball
several times, Coach VanDerveer ordered the other players to stop passing her the ball. This was the ultimate humiliation for a player like Nikki.
She lost it, and started to cry. Her teammates stepped between her and
VanDerveer to protect Nikki and let the coach know that was *enough*.

Whether this was a carefully calculated plan by the coach may never
be known, but it turned out to be the defining moment in Nikki's

Career HIGHLIGHTS

Year	Team	Achievement
1990	Colliersville H.S.	Parade All-American
1994	Tennessee	First-Team All-SEC
1994	Tennessee	SEC Player of the Year
1995	Tennessee	First-Team All-SEC
1995	Tennessee	SEC Player of the Year
1996	Team USA	Olympic Gold Medalist
1997	Columbus Quest	First-Team ABL All-Star
1997	Columbus Quest	ABL MVP
1997	Columbus Quest	ABL Champion
1998	Team USA	Gold Medalist, World Championships

basketball life, and it truly brought the team together for the first time. From that point on, Nikki developed quickly into a mature and confident performer. She soon became the team's defensive "stopper."

After the Olympics, Nikki agreed to play for the Columbus Quest of the American Basketball League. Once again, she was one of the youngest players, but she had gained a lifetime of experience playing with Team USA, and it showed.

Nikki was the heart and soul of the Quest. She played errorless defense, finished third in the ABL scoring race with 19.9 points a game, and dove all over the court for loose balls. A miserable long-range shooter in college, Nikki unveiled a polished three-pointer in the pros and used it with devastating effectiveness. "People were playing me for the drive," she smiles, "and I caught them off guard and was able to hit a lot of threes."

At the end of the year, she edged Teresa Edwards in the voting to become the league's first MVP. In a dramatic best-of-five championship series, Nikki hit a clutch shot to give Columbus a 90-89 opening-game win over the Richmond Rage. The Quest lost the next two games and teetered on the brink of elimination, but the team pulled together and beat Richmond twice to win the ABL title.

Shortly after the conclusion of the WNBA season—and just before the beginning of the ABL's second campaign—Nikki announced that she was switching leagues. She thought she could play for bigger audiences with the WNBA's new team, the Washington Mystics. She felt bad about leav-

ing her teammates in Columbus, but she suspected they would be okay. Although she was the ABL's MVP, the Quest's victory had been a team effort, with everyone contributing. As it turned out, Nikki's suspicions were correct. Without her, Columbus went on to win the 1998 ABL championship.

When the final buzzer sounded, no one in basketball was happier to see the Quest victorious than Nikki McCray.

Nikki goes up for a shot against South Korea during the 1996 Summer Olympics in Atlanta. She provided valuable scoring from the forward position.

"You have to be dedicated, you have to have desire. Basketball has to be a passion. You can't go into it for anything other than the love of the game."

Dawn Staley

When most people drive through the projects of North Philadelphia, they see danger and disintegration. When Dawn Staley drives those streets, she sees home. She grew up right on the corner of 25th Street and Diamond Avenue, and could not be any prouder. "I wouldn't change how I grew up," she says. "It was great to me. I didn't know any better and I didn't know any worse. I was just living. I never went without anything."

Dawn was born in the "City of Brotherly Love" in 1970. Her neighborhood was dominated by basketball. If there was a game—and there always was—Dawn was there. She did not care that the players were older, or that they were boys. She loved basketball, and she loved to compete. By her 10th birthday she was making teenagers look bad, and by the time she reached high school she had a reputation as one of the silkiest playmakers around. "Coming up, playing with the guys, I didn't get the chance to put the ball up as much," she says. "It's harder for me to get my shot off quick enough, so I always had to concentrate on other things. The intangibles, the things that don't show up in the stat sheets. From this I was able to develop a sixth sense for passing."

Dawn was shaped by more than the schoolyards of Philadelphia. Much credit goes to the stern-but-loving hands of her mother, Estelle, and father, Clarence. They taught important lessons to the entire family, including Dawn's sister, Tracy, and her three brothers, Lawrence, Anthony and Eric. Above all else, the Staleys emphasized the value of a good education. That was one sure way, they told their children, to get out of the projects and have a chance at a better life.

You would have to look long and hard for someone who plays basketball with as much sheer joy as Dawn.

Teresa Edwards (left) filled in for Dawn at the point when injuries limited her effectiveness during the 1996 Olympics. Their combined brilliance helped Team USA win the gold medal.

In Dawn's case, her ticket to an education was her basketball. She won a starting job as a sophomore at Dobbins Tech. As a senior, Dawn, who stood a mere 5-6, was named High School Player of the Year by USA Today—the first time the paper had honored someone less than six feet tall. When it came time to sort through all the college scholarship offers, Dawn kept in mind what her parents had always told her about getting the best education possible. She decided on the University of Virginia, which had a solid basketball program and one of the best academic reputations in the country.

There she enjoyed one of the greatest careers in college basketball history. During her four varsity seasons, the Cavaliers compiled a 110-21 record. With Dawn at the helm they won the Atlantic Coast Conference regular season title twice, and advanced to the NCAA Final Four three times. She became the first ACC player—male or female—to amass more than 2,000 points, 700 rebounds, 700 assists and 400 steals. Dawn was a three-time All-American and earned college Player of the Year honors in 1991 and '92.

Dawn was selected in 1995 by Team USA coach Tara VanDerveer as her starting point guard, but during the long tour preceding the Olympics the two women often clashed. Coach VanDerveer preferred a more conservative style of play, while Dawn liked to bring fans to their feet with creative moves and pretty passes. At times, Dawn was benched. "I've lost some playing time in the past for things I've done on the court," she admits. Sometimes they're good, sometimes they're bad. They're just instinctive. I mean, to me, that's all part of the game and I've got to do some of these things to help women's basketball grow."

Getting Personal

Dawn was born on May 4, 1970 in Philadelphia, Pennsylvania...She was a huge fan of the 76ers growing up. Her favorite player was point guard Maurice Cheeks...Dawn wears a rubber band on her right wrist during games. She snaps it whenever she makes a mistake on the court...Her great passes surprise even her teammates. Says Rage center Taj McWilliams, "You catch yourself saying, 'Whoa, how did that pass get in there?'"...If Dawn could choose a career besides basketball, she says she would consider being a Secret Service agent...Dawn's foundation is for both boys and girls. "It's for grown-ups, too," she says. "It gives people a future of hope." The foundation's after-school program has kids working with tutors on academics for one hour, and another hour on athletics.

After the Olympics, Dawn was a hot property. With two new professional leagues forming, she had been targeted as a player who could bring a little "showtime" to the women's game. Of course, there was never any doubt in her mind where she wanted to play: as soon as the American Basketball League announced it would place a team in Virginia, she was there.

In the league's first season, Dawn tallied nearly 15 points and eight assists a game for the Richmond Rage. No point guard in either league brought to the court the excitement and flair that she did. Certainly, no player was as responsible for her team's success. She dazzled the San Jose

Career *Highlights*

Year	Team	Achievement
1988	Dobbins Tech	USA Today H.S. Player of the Year
1989	Virginia	ACC Rookie of the Year
1990, 1991, 1992	Virginia	First-Team All-ACC
1991, 1992	Virginia	ACC Player of the Year
1991	Virginia	Final Four Most Outstanding Player
1991	Virginia	College Player of the Year
1996	Team USA	Olympic Gold Medalist
1997	Rage	ABL First-Team All-Star
1997	Rage	ABL Assist Champion
1998	Rage	ABL First-Team All-Star
1998	Rage	ABL 3-Point Shootout Champion
1998	Team USA	Gold Medalist, World Championships

Lasers in the playoffs, as Richmond advanced to the ABL Finals against the Columbus Quest. Player-for-player, the Quest simply had too much for Richmond. But after the Rage dropped a heartbreaker in the opening game, the team actually won the next two, with Dawn setting up teammates Taj McWilliams and Tonya Edwards again and again. In the end, Columbus prevailed, but Dawn made quite an impression. Former NBA MVP Magic Johnson was so impressed with her that he said the WNBA should do whatever it took to sign her. "She's a show-stopper," he raved. "She's what it's all about—no-look, behind-the-back, through-the-legs. They should buy that league just to get her!"

Things only got better for Dawn after the season. The Rage moved from Richmond to her hometown, Philadelphia. She could not have planned it better. One of Dawn's goals is to give back to people, to be able to support everyone in her community. That was the driving force behind the Dawn Staley Foundation. "I had an idea to start the foundation before I was selected to the Olympic team," Dawn says. "I had to wait until afterwards to get it off the ground. When I received my gold medal, I thought about other people who didn't get the opportunity to reach their goals, people in my neighborhood in particular. I just wanted to spread the wealth. I thought the best way was through a foundation."

Dawn tries to pick up a charging call on Jennifer Azzi of the San Jose Lasers during the 1998 ABL All-Star Game.

ON HER MIND

"Do I feel a responsibility to promote the game and the sport? Sure I do."

Kate Starbird

Kate Starbird knows she's a nerd. So do her friends. In fact, they call her "Bird the Nerd." She listens to country music. She took classes at Stanford University that her coach, Tara VanDerveer, said her teammates couldn't even pronounce. She drives the same old car she had in college, and she wears most of the same clothes.

But Kate doesn't mind what people think of her. In fact, she finds it kind of funny. That's because Kate is one of the most outrageously talented basketball players on the planet. She also happens to be as cool and confident as they come. "She's a wonderful player," says VanDerveer, "but to me her outstanding characteristic is an inner peace."

Kate developed her game and her easygoing personality as she bounced from town to town as an "army brat." Her father, Ed, was an officer, so Kate and the family had to move every time he was assigned to a new base. Born in West Point, NY, Kate lived at various times in Virginia, Kentucky, and Tennessee before the Starbirds settled near Tacoma, Washington, the place she now calls her hometown.

As a young girl, Kate was an outstanding athlete. That came as quite a surprise to her family, because neither of her parents—nor any of her four brothers or sisters—showed much aptitude for sports. Kate probably inherited her ability from her grandfathers, both of whom competed in the pentathlon at the 1936 Olympics. Kate's first love was soccer. She was

Kate was overjoyed at the prospect of "coming home" to play for the Seattle Reign of American Basketball League.

San Jose Lasers guard Jennifer Azzi visits with Kate before their a 1997 playoff game. Both women starred for Stanford University. Azzi was class of 1990 and Kate was class of 1997.

quick and agile, and took to the sport naturally. But she grew quickly at an early age, and soon she was too tall and gangly for soccer. It was then that she turned to basketball.

The problem was that Kate had no one to play with. She did not even know how to shoot. "No one was helping me," Kate remembers. "No one was coaching me. It took just about every bit of energy I could find to get the ball to the basket." Soon, she developed an awkward-looking "sling-shot" style, which has survived relatively unchanged to this day.

When Kate *could* find a game at the local gym it was usually with men five and six years older than she. And these games often deteriorated into hand-to-hand combat. Usually, she would practice on a far court until a group needed an extra player. She now believes that competing against stronger and faster opponents was the best thing for her.

By the time Kate first stepped on the court at Lakes High School, she was practically unstoppable. She could hit her outside shot all day if left open, and when defenders rushed to the perimeter to block her shot, she put the ball on the floor and simply blew by them. Some opponents tried to rough Kate up. At first she avoided the contact, but soon realized that this was what the other team wanted. She began to give as good as she got, and that is when she first donned her trademark knee pads for a little extra protection.

Getting Personal

Kate was born on July 30, 1975...Her name is actually pronounced "Kat-ee" ...Both of Kate's grandfathers competed in the pentathlon at the 1936 Olympics...Her mother is a writer...Kate set a PAC-10 record with 753 points during the 1996-97 season, and also became Stanford's all-time career scoring champ...The most surprising thing about pro ball to Kate is the camaraderie. "Everyone works together, and that's the most rewarding part of the game," she says. "It does consume our lives, but we don't mind. We voluntarily spend most of our time together on and off the court."...Kate helped create the first interactive sports video game to include women—NCAA March Madness '98...After basketball, Kate hopes to work for a computer company and create new software.

Kate got better and better, and by her senior year she was regarded as one of the best high school players in history. Lakes High was not a strong team, however, and could manage no better than a fifth-place finish in the state tournament. Still, Kate's heroic performance was so impressive that she still earned tourney MVP honors. Her 2,753 career points were more than any boy or girl had scored in the history of Washington high school basketball. And she was named the state's high school Player of the Year by *USA Today*. Kate made her parents proud on the academic side, too, becoming a member of the National Honor

Career Highlights

Year	Team	Achievement
1993	Lakes High	Parade All-American
1993	Lakes High	Washington Player of the Year
1994	Stanford	PAC 10 All-Freshman
1996	Stanford	PAC 10 Co-Player of the Year
1997	Stanford	PAC 10 Player of the Year
1997	Stanford	First-Team All-American
1997	Stanford	College Player of the Year

Society and a finalist for the National Merit Scholarship. She graduated with a 3.95 grade point average.

Naturally, every college in the country wanted Kate on its team. She and her parents agreed that they would look for a school with a good basketball program and great academics. Her dad pushed for Duke University, but in the end she opted for Stanford. There Kate immersed herself in her basketball and her studies. She majored in computer science and maintained a solid B+ average. Kate's marks for basketball were even better, as she made the PAC 10 All-Freshman squad and the All-Conference team as a sophomore. In her senior year, she established the school record for career points, and was the top scorer in the PAC 10. She was also a First-Team All-American and won the 1997 Naismith Award as player of the year.

Kate graduated from Stanford at just the right time. She was the nation's hottest college player when the WNBA and ABL were beginning to bid against each other for marquee talent. Kate liked the idea of playing in a league supported by the NBA, but in the end the ABL had much more to offer. Besides a higher salary, she was able to play close to home, for the Seattle Reign. "I feel lucky—really lucky to have come out of college when there were two leagues," she says. "Seattle was the place I really wanted to be." Best of all, Kate got the dream deal for every computer science nerd: an endorsement deal with Microsoft!

Kate drives to the basket against Old Dominion during the Women's Final Four in 1997.

ON HER MIND

"*Basketball is my life. It has basically changed my life. But at the same time, because of the way I was raised, family is really important to me.*"

Sheryl Swoopes

I f you have never experienced small-town Texas, the Sheryl Swoopes story might not make a whole lot of sense. Every major decision she has made—both on and off the court—has been influenced by her love of a simple, straightforward lifestyle. It is something of a minor miracle, in fact, that she became a world famous basketball star, although that had something to do with her miraculous skills.

Sheryl grew up in Brownfield in west Texas. She learned her appreciation for simple things growing up with her mother, Louise, and two brothers, James and Earl. Her father, Billy, left the family when she was an infant. Raising three children alone was a big responsibility for Sheryl's mother, but one she gladly accepted. Louise worked two jobs to make ends meet, and would have worked three if that was what it took to give her kids every opportunity to succeed.

By her 15th birthday Sheryl had grown to six feet tall. She was a sophomore at Brownfield High School, and by far the best player on the basketball team. Sheryl remembers that many of the girls she had played with during her childhood had stopped playing sports because they had gotten pregnant. Louise Swoopes made sure her daughter didn't follow the same path. "I chose not to do that," says Sheryl. "And my mom wouldn't let me do that." Not that Sheryl was lacking a social life. While she was in high school she met a fellow named Eric Jackson. They started dating and never separated. Today the two are happily married.

Sheryl laughs with teammates during a visit to the Houston Comet bench, a month after giving birth to her son, Jordan.

Sheryl Swoopes gives Jordan a good luck squeeze before taking the floor for a 1997 WNBA playoff game against the Charlotte Sting.

Sheryl led Brownfield to three consecutive state championships. The college recruiters began knocking on her door before her senior season, but everyone just assumed she would choose the University of Texas, in the state capitol of Austin. UT had a great basketball tradition, and academically it ranked with the best schools in the country. Besides, that is where the best player in the state always went, and there was no question that Sheryl was the top woman in Texas. So in the fall of 1989, she left Brownfield and headed for Austin.

Sheryl lasted exactly three days. She was miserable. She felt totally overwhelmed and completely alone. UT is a huge university, and Sheryl knew she could never be happy there. Instead, she went home and enrolled in South Plains Junior College, a small school a few miles away.

There she felt happy and comfortable, and it showed in her play. Over the next two seasons she poured in 25 points a night and averaged more than 10 rebounds. In 1991, after her second year, she was named Junior College Player of the Year.

Finally, Sheryl felt ready for the highest level of competition, and she transferred to nearby Texas Tech, which was located in the city of Lubbock. Lubbock was a lot bigger than Brown-field, but the pace of life and the people were familiar. In other words, Sheryl felt right at home. In her first year she scored 21.6 points a game and led the Lady Raiders to the Southwest Conference championship.

With Sheryl on the court, Tech had a realistic shot at the national title for the first time. That was saying a lot, considering the team had never even won a game in the NCAA Tournament. In 1992-93 the Lady Raiders repeated as SWC champs, and advanced to the finals against Ohio State. Sheryl scored a record 47 points and Texas Tech won its first national championship with a dramatic 84-82 victory. It was one of the classic individual performances in the history of basketball.

After college, Sheryl played pro ball overseas, but was homesick. She came home and worked hard to stay in shape so she could join the national team for the 1996 Olympics. She also signed a lucrative deal with Nike to to make a special women's basketball shoe.

Getting Personal

Sheryl was born on March 25, 1971..When she was eight years old she led a team called the Little Dribblers to a national tournament...Sheryl finished second in the nation in scoring with 28.1 points per game in 1992-93...Sheryl scored 53 points in a game during the 1993 SWC tournament. That broke the Reunion Arena record of 50, shared by Bernard King and Larry Bird...When Team USA played an exhibition game against Texas Tech, Sheryl not only got a standing ovation, the Lady Raiders bowed to her on the court. The school retired her number 22 the year before...The secret of Sheryl's success may be that she is never satisfied. "There's always something every day you can get better at," she says. "I just make myself come out every day and push myself."...She plays video games and shoots pool to relax between games.

Career *Highlights*

Year	Team	Achievement
1987	Brownfield H.S.	Texas State Champion
1988	Brownfield H.S.	Texas State Champion
1989	Brownfield H.S.	Texas State Champion
1991	So. Plains JC	Jr. College Player of the Year
1992	Texas Tech	SWC Player of the Year
1992	Texas Tech	First-Team All-American
1993	Texas Tech	SWC Player of the Year
1993	Texas Tech	NCAA National Champion
1993	Texas Tech	First-Team All-American
1993	Texas Tech	College Player of the Year
1994	Team USA	Goodwill Games Gold Medalist
1996	Team USA	Olympic Gold Medalist
1997	Comets	WNBA Champion

When Sheryl joined Team USA, she understood she would have to mesh her talents with players who had been through the pro basketball wars in Europe. They knew Sheryl had quit the pros after a few weeks, and they knew all about her "Air Swoopes" shoe. Some wondered whether the veterans would resent her. After all, she had received all that money and attention without really "paying her dues." As it turned out, Sheryl and her teammates got along beautifully. During the Olympics, she scored 13 points a game, and shot a sizzling 60 percent from the field.

When the Olympics ended, Sheryl faced a difficult decision. Many considered her the best player in the world, and both the ABL and WNBA wanted her badly. Once again, she went with her heart, choosing the WNBA when the league promised she would play for the Houston Comets. Houston was not exactly Brownfield, but the small towns outside the city felt a lot like home. "I'm a Texas girl, born and raised, and I want to be able to get settled in a place I can really call home," Sheryl smiles. "I want a community with my own church, my own hairdresser, my own beautician."

The WNBA season was scheduled to kick off in June of 1997, but it would start a little later for Sheryl. In January, she found out she was

Sheryl passes around Mikkio Hagiwara of the Phoenix Mercury in her WNBA debut.

pregnant with her first child. She had her son, Jordan Eric Jackson, on June 25 and returned to the Comets the first week in August—just in time to help them win the WNBA championship. It may not be an official record, but Sheryl's six-week recovery period has to be among the shortest ever. She claims she was not trying to do too much too soon—she just wanted to get back to the hardwood! "I hope that my decision to have a child and return to basketball will serve as an inspiration to working mothers everywhere," she says.

What's Next

Most people associated with the ABL and WNBA agree that, for women's basketball to take its next giant step, players will have to start doing the kinds of things that make the highlight reels on the evening news. It is hard to say, however, exactly what those "things" will be. The NBA, of course, likes to promote its above-the-rim style of play. For the time being, that does not seem to be a viable option for women's basketball. What is far more likely to happen in the short run is that ballhandling and shooting will improve, and with those improvements will come the confidence to try something new and wonderful—something that may just come to define the women's game.

Some believe that "something" will come from a player named Chamique Holdsclaw, who as a junior led the University of Tennessee to the 1998 NCAA Championship. She also won four titles with Christ the King High School in Queens, making her a seven-time champion at the tender age of 21. Holdsclaw is a 6' 1" forward who some say is already the best player in history. Holdsclaw runs the floor, pressures the ball, and rains down points on opponents, who sometimes can do no more than stand and watch in slack-jawed awe. Those who say women's basketball "needs a female Michael Jordan" may already be looking at one. She even wears number 23!

The WNBA's newest star, Nikki McCray, puts in serious practice time in preparation for a WNBA tour of Europe.

If basketball history is consistent, then it will be one individual who steps up and leads the way. That person could be in the ABL or WNBA right now, patiently waiting for her chance to shine. Perhaps she is already one of today's young stars, ready to take her game up a notch. Or she could be pushing the envelope in college. Then again, maybe she's in high school, or grade school, watching Lisa Leslie jam during the warmups and getting some interesting ideas of her own. One thing is for sure: she is out there...and when she emerges, she will be absolutely breathtaking!

INDEX

PAGE NUMBERS IN ITALICS REFER TO ILLUSTRATIONS.